# Pizza
# & Pane

# Pizza & Pane

First published in the UK in 2007 by
Apple Press
Sheridan House
114 Western Road
Hove
East Sussex
BN3 IDD
United Kingdom
www.apple-press.com


© Food Editore srl, 2005
Via Bordoni, 8 - 20124 MILANO
Via Mazzini, 6 - 43100 PARMA
www.gruppofood.com


**Thanks to:**
Alberto Rossi and Davide Di Prato (illustrations)
Simone Rugiati and Licia Cagnoni (recipes)
*I Love My House*, Barazzoni, Parma (the shop that provided the cooking utensils)
Daniele Elia and Giuseppe Venerito (recipe on page 28)
Bread: Piergiorgio Giorilli, baker and president of Richemont Club Italia;
Francesco Gualtierotti


Printed in Croatia


ISBN 978-1-84543-185-3

# Pizza & Pane

### Authentic Italian Recipes
for Every Occasion

**APPLE**

# Contents

# Basic techniques

## PIZZA & CO.: A BRIEF HISTORY

Pizzas, flat breads and tarts: all are variations of one original recipe which is the final result of countless refinements.

More than 3000 years ago, men created the first mixture of water and ground wheat grains, a simple dough that initially was just baked, then later, through the years, left to rise and baked.

The real pizza was "invented" in Naples in relatively recent times, however flat cakes and flat breads similar to pizza in their ingredients and shapes already existed in ancient Greece, in Rome and along the Mediterranean coasts long before that date.

The pizza par excellence, the most famous one, is actually the Neapolitan pizza created in the Parthenopean city between the XVIII and the XIX century. The history of Neapolitan pizza, the one with mozzarella cheese and tomato (imported to Europe after Columbus' "discovery"), is fascinating and it's almost the symbol of the vitality that has always characterized Naples and its inhabitants.

Pizza is actually a "popular" dish, entirely made of simple and poor ingredients, though very wholesome, all included in the so-called "Mediterranean diet". Pizza was cooked in the numerous city bakeries then directly sold in the streets or "home delivered".

There's a famous anecdote about the "Pizza Margherita" recipe: tradition says that in 1889 the pizza maker

Raffaele Esposito prepared this pizza for the Italian Queen Margherita. He topped it with mozzarella cheese, tomato and basil, maybe in honour of the Italian flag, and then dedicated his "creation" to the Queen.

Even the spread of pizza outside Naples is characteristic and tied to Italian history. Pizza has been exported to the United States and to many other countries by those pizza makers who, emigrating in search of better living conditions, brought with them the Neapolitan "secret" and clearly met with a huge success. Today, despite regional differences and newly born traditions, pizza is by far one of the most popular dishes in the world. It's baked and eaten all over the world, and actually wherever you go, you can pronounce the word "pizza" without fearing being misunderstood.

## NUTRITIONAL CHARACTERISTICS

Pizzas, flat breads and tarts have partially the same nutritional characteristics of bread, the primary source of carbohydrates which are fundamental in a balanced diet.

Pizza is a complete food with a correct proportion of lipids, proteins, sugars, fibres, salts and vitamins, particularly when vegetables and cheese are mixed with tomatoes, anchovies and oregano.

The traditional pizza "Margherita" contains the elements for a balanced meal: flour carbohydrates, tomato vitamins and mozzarella proteins, all seasoned with a drizzle of extra virgin olive oil. From a nutritional point of view, the best recipe is the one with vegetables, as it completes the meal with vitamins, minerals and fibres making the carbohydrates to digest easier.

Be careful however not to over-indulge with extra toppings as this alters pizza from a nutritional standpoint, unbalancing its values.

Pizza is also easily digestible thanks to the action of starches and a correct rising that, together with baking, is a fundamental element for digestibility. Pizza is the ideal choice for lunch: carbohydrates burn quickly and are easily assimilated.

The same is also true for flat breads, savoury pies and sandwiches. Dishes like these are balanced, varied and complete in their composition. In other words, a Margherita, a "vegetarian" pizza or any source of carbohydrates (such as bread, focaccia, savoury pie or tart) with a simple and wholesome topping is the ideal compromise between taste and good health.

## BASIC INGREDIENTS

**Flour** - Wheat flour is used for the pizza base because it is easy to knead and makes the dough soft and elastic. You can also use a bit of Manitoba flour or "strong" flour, which contain many proteins and are suited for long rising processes. An alternative is the pizza flour which already contains the right mixture of both flours and is available in the best supermarkets.

**Water** - Here temperature is important, because it affects the rising speed. If water is too cold, especially in winter, it hinders the dough rising. On the other hand, if water is too hot, it accelerates the rising process too much and the dough turns out less elastic. The ideal water temperature is about 22°C/72°F in winter and 18°C/64°F in summer.

**Yeasts** - These are living micro-organisms that produce gases needed for dough fermentation. Fresh Brewer's yeast is more suited for home-made pizza but it only keeps for a short time. Alternatively, you can use dry granular yeast, taking care to dissolve it in lukewarm water before mixing with flour (as you do for fresh yeast).

**Tomato** - Tomatoes are a typical ingredient of pizza. According to the traditional recipe, peeled tomatoes are

first puréed, seasoned with oil, salt, pepper and oregano and then spread onto the pizza base before baking. Some people suggest adding a teaspoon of sugar to the purée, in order to take its acid taste away. In summer you may like to use diced fresh tomatoes instead of pulped ones.

## Pizza
Ingredients
(700g/1lb 9 oz dough)

300g/11oz/2 cups plain white flour
200g/7oz/1 cup strong white flour
1 block of Brewer's yeast (16g/½oz/1 tbsp)
250ml/9fl oz/1 cup water
4 tbsp extra virgin olive oil
1 tsp sugar
2 tsp salt

### Preparation
Dissolve crumbled yeast in lukewarm water. Add salt, sugar and oil; mix energically using a wooden spoon. Sift both flours and mould them in a well shape, then pour the mixture.

Flour a large plastic bowl; knead the dough thoroughly, flour generously and leave it to rise in the bowl, covered with a kitchen cloth. Leave to rest for approximately 2 hours, then knead the dough again just to shape it into single-portion balls and leave them to rise under a cloth for 1 hour.

### Variations
If you like a browner and crispier crust, add an egg yolk to the dough.

You may like to vary the base of your pizza by adding 150g/5½oz/1 cup of boiled and mashed potatoes to 500g/1lb 2oz/3¼ cups of flour. This dough is particularly suited for panfried pizzas and flat breads.

Too much salt hinders dough fermentation. Add a tablespoon of malt or a pinch of sugar to support the rising process and give the dough an unusual taste.

Wholemeal pizza: Mix 500g/1lb 2oz/3¼ cups of wholemeal flour, 1½ tbsp of Brewer's yeast, 2 tbsp of olive oil and salt. Knead for 10 minutes adding enough water to make a smooth dough that easily comes away from the worktop.

Shape the dough into a ball and let it rise in a warm place for approximately 1.5 hours.

## Tips

If you have an oven with separate temperatures, heat the lower rack to 230°C/450°F/Gas 8 and the upper rack to 220°C/425°F/Gas 7 so that the base, which requires longer baking, cooks evenly and the surface doesn't burn.

## Cooking

Speaking of wood-fired ovens, electric ovens and personal preferences, we must point out that these kinds of ovens, used in pizzerias, reach temperatures that home ovens usually don't. On a baking surface, at 300-350°C/570°F-660°F, pizza takes about 10 minutes to be evenly baked, while in home ovens cooking can require more than 20 minutes with obvious consequences on the rising of the pizza.

Because of high temperatures and very quick cooking, wood-fired ovens are particularly suited to bake thin pizzas, while home ovens are usually more suited for thick pizzas.

There are those who suggest putting a small saucepan with about 1 litre/1¾ pints/4 cups of water in the oven together with the pizza pan: this will prevent the dough from becoming too dry.

While rolling out the dough in the pan, remember to spread tomato sauce at once and to only add mozzarella on it halfway through the cooking, to avoid burning your pizza.

## Focaccia (flat bread)

Focaccia is the closest relative of pizza, perhaps its distant forerunner. If pizza was supposedly invented to "improve" a focaccia topping, today flat breads offer tasty and extravagant recipes that heighten a chef's inspiration and creativity. Flat breads can't substitute for a complete meal, however they are the best choice for a tasty snack.

## Ingredients

(700g/1lb 9oz bread)
500g/1lb 2 oz/3¼ cups strong white flour
25g/1oz/1½ tbsp Brewer's yeast
50g/2oz/¼ cup butter
oil or bread seasoning
1 tsp salt

## Preparation

Dissolve the yeast in a little water, add the remaining ingredients and knead thoroughly to get a dough of medium texture. Leave it to rest in a warm place, covered or oiled, for approximately 15 minutes.

Cut the dough into pieces of required weight, shape them into balls and leave to rest again for a few minutes. Arrange the dough balls on a baking tray, flatten them and pour over the remaining oil. Wait 30 minutes for the dough to rise, then bake at 250°C/480°F/Gas 9 without damping. Cooking times vary according to the focaccia thickness and size.

## Variations

If you like a much tastier and richer focaccia, use lard instead of butter.

## Tips

If you want a thicker focaccia to fill, bake it at a temperature 30°C/86°F lower than the recommended one and, after 10 minutes, reduce it again. This gives the yeasts more time to swell the dough.

## Puff pastry

Light and crumbly, puff pastry is the ideal "base" for many recipes.

### Ingredients

(500g/1lb 2oz pastry)
200g/7oz/1 cup plain white flour
250g/9oz/1 cup margarine
100ml/3½fl oz/½ cup water
a pinch of salt

### Preparation

Pour the flour into a pile, make a well in the middle then add water and salt. Work the dough with your hands, wrap it in a kitchen cloth and leave to rest for 20 minutes. Using a rolling pin, flatten the dough until you get a 5mm/¼in thick square. Place the finely crumbled margarine in the middle, fold over the dough and close it completely, as to form a parcel. Flatten gently using a rolling pin, wrap the dough in aluminium foil and allow to rest in the fridge for 5 minutes.

First "step": Place the dough again on the worktop and roll it out into a long strip (about 1cm/½in thick). Fold it up in three portions (fold one third towards the middle and cover it with the remaining third, to form three layers), then turn it round 90°.

Second "step": Roll the dough into a long strip, fold it up

again in three portions, wrap in aluminium foil and keep in the fridge for approximately 30 minutes.

Repeat these steps twice more, 6 "steps" in all. After the last "step" leave the puff pastry to rest in the fridge for almost 1 hour, then use it as a base for your recipe.

## Piadina

Piadina is the most popular focaccia in Romagna and boasts unsuspected origins: first testimonies go back to the Middle Ages. Piadina is great with salami, cheese and vegetables. As for flat breads and savoury pies, toppings have just one limit: your taste or your fantasy.

### Ingredients

500g/1lb 2oz/3¼ cups plain white flour
3 tbsp lard
1 cup water
salt

## Preparation

Pour the flour into a pile on a worktop. Dissolve the lard in 200ml/7fl oz/1 cup of warm water and add a generous pinch of salt.

Make a well in the middle of the flour, add the lard-salt mix and begin working the paste with your fingertips. Mix and knead to form a smooth and elastic ball.

If necessary, add lukewarm water. The dough must be slightly fluffier than egg pasta. Wrap in clingfilm and leave to rest at room temperature.

Flatten the dough gradually using a rolling pin and make it about 3 mm/$^1$/$_8$ in thick. Place piadinas on a hot cast-iron hob plate and cook for about 3 minutes per side. Turn piadinas as soon as they are nicely browned.

## Variations

For a more puffed piadina, add 1 teaspoon of bicarbonate and a drizzle of olive oil in the dough.

## Tips

It is the pastry thinness that makes a piadina so crispy: the thinner the pastry is, the crispier the piadina will be.

## Panzerotto

Once again Naples is protagonist: the name "panzerotto" was coined in the Parthenopean city. "Panzerotti" however is also the name of a type of pasta and of potato croquettes.

As well as pizza, panzerotto is very popular, with slight variations, in the Mediterranean region.

## Ingredients

(300g/11oz panzerotto)
200g/7oz/1 cup plain white flour
½ block of Brewer's yeast (8g/¼oz/½ tbsp)
100ml/3½fl oz/½ cup water
1 tbsp extra virgin olive oil
salt

## Preparation

Crumble the Brewer's yeast in lukewarm water and stir until it is fully dissolved. Add a generous pinch of salt and the extra virgin olive oil. Pour the mixture on the sifted flour and work the dough with your fingertips

in order to mix the ingredients. Continue to knead energically until the dough is smooth and leave it to rise under a damp cloth in a warm place for approximately 30 minutes.

## Variations
Flavour the panzerotto dough with a mixture of finely chopped aromatic herbs or with a mixture of walnuts or pistachios.

## Tips
If you have no time or no yeast, you can use baking powder for pizza (½ tbsp), being careful to dissolve it in cold water.

## Bread
Food par excellence, bread boasts a very ancient history.

Perhaps, the two elements that most distinguish modern bread from ancient bread are the rising process and the use of "soft" wheat. The Egyptians created the first "modern" bread in history: from this cultured civilization bread spread to the Mediterranean area.

Bread made its first appearance in Rome relatively late (in the II century BC, even if, in former times, people used to eat flat breads and various mixtures).

Different types of bread already existed in Greece at least a century before that date.

Today it's almost impossible to live without bread

baked in many different ways and available in many different shapes. For example, variuos types of leavened bread are to be found in north Italy (it seems to be a Celtic legacy), while in central and south Italy (islands included) bread often takes unusual and bizarre shapes: thin bread with rustic shapes is quite common.

Here is the basic recipe for bread.

## Ingredients
(700g/1lb 9 oz bread)
500g/1lb 2oz/3¼ cups plain white flour
100g/3½oz/½ cup butter
25g/1oz/1½ tbsp Brewer's yeast
water
salt

## Preparation
Prepare a dough with yeast, 2 tablespoons of flour and water, then work the dough until smooth.

On the top of the dough make a cruciform incision and leave to rise until it doubles in volume.

Meanwhile, knead the remaining flour, the butter, a pinch of salt and water. Mix the ingredients and add the risen dough, work the pastry energically until little bubbles appear on the surface.

Make a cruciform incision on the top and leave the dough to rise until it doubles in volume.

# Pizzas

Tasty and crispy pizzas
topped with simple and
extravagant ingredients.
Many ideas to present
this classic of Italian cuisine
in a new and creative way.

# Calabrese pizza with capers and aubergines

Serves 4

### Dough
300g/11oz pizza dough

### Topping
1 aubergine
1 tbsp capers, drained and rinsed
280g/10oz/1¼ cup buffalo mozzarella, diced
20 cherry tomatoes
3 tbsp extra virgin olive oil
basil, torn
salt and pepper

**Preparation time:** 20 minutes
**Cooking time:** 15 minutes
**Difficulty:** easy
**Beer:** Italian Lager

Divide the pizza dough (see instructions on page 9) into 4 balls (if you like round pizzas, otherwise stretch the dough in an oiled rectangular baking tray). Leave to rise under a damp cloth.

Wash the aubergine, cut it into thin round slices, heat a ridged grill pan and grill the aubergine slices for 2 minutes per side. Wash the tomatoes and cut them into 4 segments.

Roll out the dough balls until thin and sprinkle with mozzarella cheese, capers and tomatoes; season with oil, salt and pepper and bake at 230°C/450°F/Gas 8 for 8 minutes.

Halfway through the cooking, add the aubergine slices and continue to bake until the edges are nicely browned and crispy. Remove from the oven, sprinkle with fresh basil leaves and serve immediately.

**Cook's tip -** If you like a well-risen pizza, roll out the dough in an oiled baking tray, sprinkle with tomatoes, capers and mozzarella cheese and leave to rise in a warm place; bake at 220°C/425°F/Gas 7 for 12 minutes.

# Pizza with fresh tomatoes and artichoke hearts

**Serves 4**

### *Dough*
240g/8½oz pizza dough

### *Topping*
2 red tomatoes
350g/12oz/1½ cups buffalo mozzarella, diced
200g/7oz/1 cup artichoke hearts in oil, cut into segments
2 tbsp extra virgin olive oil
basil
salt and pepper

**Preparation time:** 15 minutes
**Cooking time:** 10 minutes
**Difficulty:** easy
**Beer:** Italian Lager

Wash the tomatoes and dry with kitchen paper towel; cut them into thin segments and set aside.

Drain the artichoke hearts and dry on several kitchen paper towels. Wash and thoroughly wipe the basil.

On a floured surface, roll out the dough (see instructions on page 9) until thin and top with mozzarella cheese and tomato segments. Season with extra virgin olive oil, salt and pepper.

Add the artichoke hearts; bake at 230°C/450°F/Gas 8 for 8 minutes. Remove from the oven and sprinkle with fresh basil leaves. Serve hot.

# Earth and sea pizza

Serves 4

**Dough**

280g/10oz pizza dough

**Topping**

4 mushrooms
200g/7oz/1 cup mozzarella cheese, diced
20 black olives, stoned, drained and rinsed
15 shrimp tails, peeled and deveined
1 bunch of rocket
3 tbsp extra virgin olive oil
salt and pepper

**Preparation time:** 20 minutes
**Cooking time:** 15 minutes
**Difficulty:** easy
**Beer:** Irish Stout

Divide the dough into 4 balls (see instructions on page 9) and leave to rise under a damp cloth in a warm place.

Peel the mushrooms and discard the earthy bottom of their stems. Wash the rocket and dry it in a salad spinner or with kitchen paper towels.

Roll out the dough until thin and sprinkle with mozzarella cheese, shrimp tails, black olives, finely sliced mushrooms, oil, salt and pepper.

Bake at 230°C/450°F/Gas 8 for about 8 minutes, then top with the chopped rocket; season again with a drizzle of oil and a pinch of salt. Serve hot.

# Pizza with broad beans, pecorino cheese and bacon

Serves 4

### Dough
240g/8½oz pizza dough

### Topping
250g/9oz/1 cup pecorino cheese, finely diced
300g/11oz/1½ cups broad beans
150g/5½oz/¾ cup streaky bacon, thinly sliced
3 tbsp extra virgin olive oil
salt and black pepper

**Preparation time:** 20 minutes
**Cooking time:** 10 minutes
**Difficulty:** easy
**Beer:** Czech Republic Pilsner

Divide the dough (see instructions on page 9) into 4 balls and leave to rise under a damp cloth.

Blanch the broad beans in salted boiling water for 1 minute, drain and rinse in cold water. Shell them keeping only their heart and set aside.

Using a rolling pin, roll out or stretch the dough on a floured surface giving it a round shape; sprinkle with broad beans and pecorino cheese. Season with a drizzle of olive oil, salt and black pepper.

Bake at 240°C/475°F/Gas 9 for about 6 minutes; remove from the oven as soon as the pizza base becomes crispy. Sprinkle with bacon slices and serve.

**Note -** The bacon fat melts beacuse of the pizza heat, releasing a particular taste. The ingredients are those used for recipes traditionally prepared in Tuscany for May Day celebrations.

BACON
Bacon is produced in many regions of the world using the fatty tissue of the pig belly. It comes in a wide variety of cuts: "streaky bacon" is stretched, trimmed, salted and left to mature or smoked; "rolled bacon" is obtained from the leanest parts that are pickled, rolled up and tied.
There's also the so-called "pancetta coppata" which is rolled up with a bit of the pig back (near the head).

# Pizza with mushrooms and sausage

**Serves 4**

### Dough
400g/14oz/2¾ cups plain white flour
200ml/7fl oz/1 cup water
1/2 block of Brewer's yeast
3 tbsp extra virgin olive oil
1 tsp sugar
salt

### Topping
180g/6½oz/1 cup peeled tomatoes
220g/7½oz/1 cup mozzarella cheese
2 sausages, skin removed and crumbled
6 fresh mushrooms
3 tbsp extra virgin olive oil
salt and pepper

**Preparation time:** 20 minutes
**Cooking time:** 25 minutes
**Difficulty:** easy
**Beer:** Italian Lager

Prepare the pizza dough following the instructions on page 9. Thoroughly wash the mushrooms and cut them into thin slices.

Purée the tomatoes with a pinch of salt and pepper. Roll out the dough into 4 small oiled tins and pour a little tomato purée in the middle of the dough spreading it all over the pizza top with the back of a spoon, leaving 1cm/½in round the edge.

Pass the mozzarella cheese through a mincer or dice it, spread it on the pizza surface and top with the sausages and mushrooms. Season the pizzas with a drizzle of oil, salt and pepper and bake at 220°C/425°F/Gas 7 for about 25 minutes. Remove from the oven and serve hot.

**Tip -** If you prefer a more delicate taste, season this pizza with a drizzle of truffle oil just before serving.

# Pizza with rocket and cherry tomatoes

**Serves 4**

### *Dough*
400g/14oz pizza dough

### *Topping*
300g/11oz/1½ cups mozzarella cheese, diced
20 cherry tomatoes
2 bunches of rocket
150g/5½oz/1 cup Parmesan cheese
3 tbsp extra virgin olive oil
salt

**Preparation time:** 10 minutes
**Cooking time:** 15 minutes
**Difficulty:** easy
**Beer:** Pilsner

On a floured surface, roll out the dough (see instructions on page 9) until thin. Sprinkle mozzarella cheese on the pizza base.

Wash the cherry tomatoes, slice them in half and arrange over the mozzarella.

Add salt and bake at 220°C/425°F/Gas 7 for 15 minutes. Meanwhile, wash, dry and chop the rocket.

Before serving, sprinkle rocket and Parmesan flakes on the pizza and season with olive oil.

**Cook's tip -** You may like to vary this classical recipe mixing mozzarella cheese with some sweet provola. This cheese is less watery so it doesn't leave the base wet and the pizza turns out crispier. The taste will also be stronger.

# Delicate pizza with truffle oil

**Serves 4**

**_Dough_**
300g/11oz pizza dough

**_Topping_**
250g/9oz/1 cup Fior di latte mozzarella, diced or finely sliced
2 porcini mushrooms (or 120g/4oz/1 cup mushrooms in oil)
150g/5oz/1 cup Parmesan cheese
3 tbsp truffle oil
salt and pepper

**_Preparation time:_** 10 minutes
**_Cooking time:_** 10 minutes
**_Difficulty:_** easy
**_Beer:_** English Pale Ale

Remove the earthy bottom of the mushroom stems and thoroughly wipe them with damp kitchen towels.

Cut the mushrooms in 2 pieces lengthwise then thinly slice them (if you use mushrooms in oil, simply drain them and dry on kitchen towels).

Roll out the dough (see instructions on page 9) shaping it into 4 thin discs, season with truffle oil and a pinch of salt. Sprinkle with mozzarella cheese and mushroom slices.

Dust with Parmesan flakes obtained with a mandoline slicer or a peeler. Add a little salt and bake at 230°C/450°F/Gas 8 for about 8 minutes. Serve hot.

**Note -** The truffle oil fragrance emanates bite after bite and, together with porcini, it creates a bouquet of tastes and aromas that bring the smell of wood to mind.

# Pizza with truffle, provola cheese and cooked ham

**Serves 4**

### Dough
280g/10oz pizza dough

### Topping
250g/9oz/1 cup sweet provola cheese
180g/6½oz cooked ham
1 small black truffle, finely sliced
100g/3½oz/½ cup mozzarella cheese
2 tbsp delicate extra virgin olive oil
salt

**Preparation time:** 10 minutes
**Cooking time:** 12 minutes
**Difficulty:** easy
**Beer:** German Weizen

Divide the dough into 4 balls and leave to rise (see instructions on page 9) in a warm place under a damp cloth.

Thinly slice the provola cheese or process it together with mozzarella in a mincer.

Scrub the truffle with a brush to remove possible earthy pieces. Dice the cooked ham or take some slices and cut them into small strips.

Stretch or roll out the dough on a floured surface, making it as thin as possible, then sprinkle with mozzarella and provola. Season the edges with a little oil and salt, arrange the ham and bake at 240°C/475°F/Gas 9 for 8 minutes.

Remove the pizza from the oven as soon as the edges are nicely browned and crispy. Arrange in serving plates, sprinkle with truffle and serve immediately.

**Note -** The delicacy and the intense taste of sweet provola cheese merge with the powerful smell of black truffle creating a rich and sophisticated flavour.

### COOKED HAM
To obtain the best ham, simply bone some gammon pork, pickle and steam it in appropriate moulds.
Once cooled, the ham is left to mature for a few days then it's ready to reach the supermarket shelves.

# Classic pizza regina

**Serves 4-6**

### Dough
400g/14oz/2¾ cups plain white flour
200ml/7fl oz/1 cup water
½ block of Brewer's yeast
3 tbsp extra virgin olive oil
1 tsp sugar
salt

### Topping
4 tomatoes, peeled
2 tbsp extra virgin olive oil
200g/7oz/1 cup mozzarella cheese
salt

### To garnish
20 cherry tomatoes, cut into segments
basil

**Preparation time:** 10 minutes
**Cooking time:** 20 minutes
**Difficulty:** easy
**Beer:** Italian Lager

Prepare the pizza dough following the instructions on page 9. Roll out the dough until about 0.5cm/¼in thick, using a rolling pin and line 4 tins greased with a drizzle of olive oil.

Purée the tomatoes, cut the mozzarella cheese into small dices and dry them with kitchen paper towels.

Spread tomatoes and mozzarella cheese on the pizzas, season with a drizzle of olive oil and a pinch of salt.

Bake at 200°C/400°F/Gas 6 for about 20 minutes. Remove from the oven and garnish with fresh tomatoes and some basil leaves. Serve immediately so that pizzas are still fragrant.

**Cook's tip -** To make a much tastier pizza, add black olives, capers, some anchovy fillets and basil. Serve immediately so that pizza is still fragrant.

# Thick pizza with turnip greens

Serves 4

### *Dough*
400g/14oz pizza dough

### *Topping*
2 Neapolitan sausages
1 bunch of turnip greens
2 cloves of garlic, crushed
½ red chilli, crumbled
3 tbsp extra virgin olive oil
salt and pepper

**Preparation time:** 20 minutes
**Cooking time:** 25 minutes
**Difficulty:** easy
**Beer:** English Pale Ale

Remove the leaves of the turnip greens and wash them in cold water; drain and set aside.

Heat a saucepan filled with a little water and cook the sausages (with their skin) for about 5 minutes to skim their fat. Brown the garlic quickly with oil and chilli.

Add the turnip greens (still wet) and cover. Cook for 5 minutes stirring occasionally; cut the sausages in 2 parts and put them in. Season to taste with salt and pepper and cook for 8 more minutes.

Stretch or roll the dough (see instructions on page 9), leaving it rather thick, and allow to rise in a greased tin in a warm place. Sprinkle turnip greens and lightly crumbled sausages on the dough; bake at 220°C/425°F/Gas 7 for about 12 minutes. Remove from the oven and serve hot.

**Cook's tip -** If you like a much tastier and stringier pizza, mix thinly sliced mozzarella into the dough.

# Pizza with radicchio and Parmesan cheese

**Serves 4-6**

### *Dough*
300g/11oz/2 cups plain wheat flour
100g/3½oz/¾ cup strong wheat flour
20g/¾oz/1 tbsp Brewer's yeast
150ml/5fl oz/⅔ cup water
3 tbsp extra virgin olive oil
salt

### *Topping*
400g/14oz/2 cups red radicchio, thinly sliced
150g/5oz/1 cup Parmesan cheese
2-3 tbsp balsamic vinegar
4 tbsp extra virgin olive oil
1 tbsp parsley, chopped
salt and pepper

**Preparation time:** 15 minutes
**Cooking time:** 30 minutes
**Difficulty:** easy
**Beer:** Belgian White

In a bowl, dissolve the yeast in a little lukewarm water. Add oil, 2 tablespoons of flour and stir until thick; leave to rise in a warm place for 30 minutes.

Pour both flours into a pastry board, place the block of yeast in the middle, add salt and gradually pour in lukewarm water until the dough becomes soft. Knead energically for 10 minutes, shape the dough into a ball, lightly flour it and cover with a cloth. Leave to rise in a warm place for about 2 hours.

Divide the dough into 2 portions and, using a rolling pin, roll out or stretch them until you get 2 discs (0.5cm/¼in thick). Line 2 baking tins, leaving an overlapping edge, then brush with oil. Bake at 200°C/400°F/Gas 6 for 15 minutes.

Wash the radicchio, stir-fry in a saucepan with 2 tablespoons of oil and a pinch of salt. Sprinkle with balsamic vinegar then add the parsley. Spread the radicchio on the pizza and bake it again for 10 minutes. Dust with Parmesan flakes and pepper then season with extra virgin olive oil.

# Potato mini pizzas with grilled vegetables and cherry tomatoes

**Serves 4**

### Dough
250g/9oz/1 cup plain white flour
120g/4oz/1 cup potatoes (boiled and mashed)
100ml/3½fl oz/½ cup milk
½ tbsp Brewer's yeast
2 tbsp extra virgin olive oil

### Topping
150g/5oz/1 cup aubergines and courgettes in oil
150g/5oz/1 cup cherry tomatoes
150g/5oz/1 cup buffalo mozzarella, diced
oregano
salt and pepper

**Preparation time:** 15 minutes
**Cooking time:** 20 minutes
**Difficulty:** easy
**Beer:** Italian Lager

Dissolve the yeast in the milk, then add all the other ingredients and knead until the dough becomes smooth. Shape it into a ball, cover with a kitchen cloth and leave to rise for about 1 hour.

Meanwhile, arrange cherry tomatoes on a baking tray, brush with oil, dust with salt, pepper and oregano. Bake at 180°C/350°F/Gas 4 for 15 minutes.

Roll out the dough and cut it into small rings of 8cm/3¼in in diameter, arrange them on a baking tray and leave to rise for 15 minutes.

Bake the mini pizzas at 190°C/375°F/Gas 5 for 15 minutes, sprinkle vegetables, oregano and mozzarella cheese on each pizza then bake again for 5 minutes.

**Cook's tip -** If you want a richer taste, top the mini pizzas with mozzarella cheese, a drizzle of basil pesto, onions cooked with thyme, grilled peppers, goats cheese, cubes of avocado pear and tomato.

# Spicy pizza with turnip greens

Serves 4-6

### *Dough*
300g/11oz/2 cups plain wheat flour
100g/3½oz/¾ cup strong wheat flour
1 tbsp Brewer's yeast
150ml/5fl oz/⅔ cup water
3 tbsp extra virgin olive oil
salt

### *Topping*
400g/14oz/2 cups turnip greens
2 cloves of garlic, thinly sliced
150g/5oz/1 cup buffalo mozzarella, diced
4 tbsp extra virgin olive oil
chilli
salt

**Preparation time:** 30 minutes
**Cooking time:** 30 minutes
**Difficulty:** easy
**Beer:** German Weizen

In a bowl, dissolve the yeast in a little lukewarm water. Add 2 tablespoons of flour and stir to make a thick batter; leave to rise in a warm place for 30 minutes.

Pour both flours onto a pastry board making a well in the centre, place the yeast block in the middle, add salt and gradually pour in lukewarm water until you get a soft dough. Knead energically for 10 minutes, shape the dough into a ball, slightly flour it and cover with a cloth. Leave to rise in a warm place for about 2 hours.

Using a rolling pin, stretch the dough until you get a 0.5cm/¼in thick rectangle that fits in the baking tray.

Brush the pan with oil, line it with the dough and leave an overlapping edge around. Wash the turnip greens and simmer them in a saucepan with the oil, garlic cloves and chilli. Add salt and a little water, cover and cook for 10 minutes, until the turnip greens are dry and tender.

Spread the turnip greens on the dough, sprinkle with mozzarella cheese and bake at 200°C/400°F/Gas 6 for 20 minutes.

## CHILLI
From a botanical point of view, pepper and chilli plants are very similar; the main difference, besides the fruit size, is the higher quantity of capsaicin (the active component that gives chilli its characteristic spicy taste).

# Pizza with sweet vegetables

**Serves 4**

### *Dough*
200g/7oz/1 cup wholemeal flour
200g/7oz/1 cup white flour
1 block of Brewer's yeast
200ml/7fl oz/1 cup water
4 tbsp extra virgin olive oil
½ tsp sugar
salt and pepper

### *Vegetables*
1 red onion, sliced
1 courgette, thinly sliced
½ yellow pepper, cut into small strips
½ red pepper, cut into small strips
extra virgin olive oil
salt and pepper

**Preparation time:** 20 minutes
**Cooking time:** 30 minutes
**Difficulty:** easy
**Beer:** Belgian White

Dissolve Brewer's yeast and sugar in lukewarm water, then knead with the flours. Add extra virgin olive oil and prepare the dough; allow to rest for 2 hours.

Stretch or roll the dough, leaving it rather thick. Arrange all the vegetables on the pizza and season with extra virgin olive oil, salt and pepper. Leave to rise again for 1 hour and bake at 190°C/375°F/Gas 5 for 20 minutes. Serve hot.

# Savoury pies

Delicious recipes to prepare savoury
pies and flans of great success.
Amaze your guests and satisfy even
the most demanding palates with fish,
meat, cheese or vegetable pies.

# Pumpkin wholemeal flan with pecorino cheese, nuts and basil

**Serves 4**

### *Pastry*
150g/5oz/1 cup plain white flour
150g/5oz/1 cup wholemeal flour
3 tbsp pumpkin seeds, finely chopped
50ml/2fl oz/¼ cup water
1 block of Brewer's yeast

### *Stuffing*
2 eggs
100ml/3½fl oz/½ cup milk
150g/5oz/1 cup sweet pecorino cheese
2 carrots, peeled and cut into julienne strips
1 tsp potato flour
a handful of salted pistachios, chopped
salt and pepper

**Preparation time:** 25 minutes
**Cooking time:** 45 minutes
**Difficulty:** easy
**Wine:** Riviera Ligure di Ponente Pigato

Dissolve the Brewer's yeast in lukewarm water; sift both flours and knead with yeast. Blend in the pumpkin seeds and let rise for approximately 30 minutes.

Meanwhile, beat the eggs, milk, pecorino cheese and potato flour together. Season to taste with salt and pepper.

Roll out the pastry until thin, line an oven mould then fill with the carrots and the beaten mixture. Dust with chopped pistachios. Bake at 190°C/375F°/Gas 5 for 45 minutes and serve hot.

# Courgette and escarole pie

**Serves 4**

### *Pastry*
250g/9oz filo pastry
1 head of escarole
2 courgettes, sliced
1 clove of garlic
2 tbsp extra virgin olive oil
salt and pepper

***Preparation time:*** 20 minutes
***Cooking time:*** 25 minutes
***Difficulty:*** easy
***Wine:*** Vermentino di Gallura

Lightly crush the garlic without peeling it and heat in a saucepan with extra virgin olive oil.

Wash the escarole in several changes of water, chop it coarsely and stew for 10 minutes with the garlic. Remove the garlic, then season with salt and pepper to taste.

Separate the five filo pastry sheets and lay out three of them in a lightly greased baking tray. Add the well-drained escarole and top with courgettes.

Season with a drizzle of olive oil, salt and pepper. Cover with the remaining filo pastry sheets and bake at 200°C/400°F/Gas 6 for 12-15 minutes. Serve hot.

# Pea flan with black olives and pine nuts

**Serves 4**

### *Pâte brisée*
300g/11oz/1½ cups plain white flour
150 g/5oz/¾ cup butter, lightly softened and diced
900ml/3¾ cups water
salt

### *Stuffing*
400g/14oz/2 cups peas
1 onion
1 tbsp extra virgin olive oil
vegetable stock
1 egg
10 black olives, stoned
a handful of pine nuts
salt and pepper

**Preparation time:** 30 minutes
**Cooking time:** 55 minutes
**Difficulty:** easy
**Wine:** Alto Adige Sylvaner

Pour the flour into a pile onto a pastry board, add a pinch of salt and make a well in the middle. Add the butter and slowly pour in cold water. Knead until the pâte brisée becomes smooth and white; wrap it in clingfilm and allow to rest in the fridge for 20 minutes.

Meanwhile, chop the onion and fry it gently in oil. Add the peas, pour in the vegetable stock and cook for 15 minutes. Process the mixture in a food processor and leave to cool. Season to taste with salt and pepper.

Add the egg and mix gently, then blend in the black olives. Roll out the pâte brisée until thin and line a baking tin. Fill with the filling, garnish with pine nuts and bake at 180°C/350°F/Gas 4 for 40 minutes.

# Vegetable triangles

**Serves 4-6**

### *Triangles*

10 brick pastry sheets
250g/9oz/1 cup pumpkin, chopped
200g/7oz/1 cup peas
1 onion
1 clove of garlic
1 bay leaf
100ml/3½fl oz/½ cup water
1 tbsp extra virgin olive oil
1 tbsp coriander
a pinch of ginger powder
1 tsp turmeric
1 egg yolk
oil for deep-frying
salt and pepper

**Preparation time:** 10 minutes
**Cooking time:** 50 minutes
**Difficulty:** easy
**Wine:** Prosecco di Conegliano
e Valdobbiadene Brut

Thinly slice the onion and fry it with garlic and oil. Pour in the water and shortly afterwards add the peas and the pumpkin. Add the spices and cook for about 30 minutes, until the mixture becomes tender and well mixed. Leave to cool and remove the bay leaf. Cut the brick pastry sheets in half.

Place one tablespoon of stuffing on each half sheet. Fold the pastry over into a triangle; seal the edges brushing with egg yolk and pressing down gently until they perfectly adhere.

Heat a saucepan with a generous amount of oil and fry the triangles on a high heat, turning over until they are nicely browned.

**Note -** Brick pastry is a very light puff pastry used in Arabic and North-African cuisine for preparing meat, vegetable or fish dishes but also for desserts. If you can't find it, use filo pastry.

# Pumpkin and radicchio pie

**Serves 6**

### Pie

250g/9oz puff pastry
250g/9oz pâte brisée
½ pumpkin, peeled, seeded and diced
1/2 red radicchio of Chioggia, cut into small strips
250g/9oz/1 cup peas
2 tbsp sesame seeds
1 tbsp sunflower seeds
1 onion
3 tbsp extra virgin olive oil
1 egg
salt and pepper

**Preparation time:** 25 minutes
**Cooking time:** 45 minutes
**Difficulty:** easy
**Wine:** Lugana

Thinly slice half of the onion, add a drizzle of oil and the pumpkin. Pour in 100ml/3fl oz of water and cook for 10 minutes.

Cut the remaining onion into thin slices, add a drizzle of olive oil and red radicchio; leave to cook for a couple of minutes. Meanwhile, blanch the peas in hot and salted water for 2 minutes.

Process the pumpkin in a food processor and add peas and radicchio. Add an egg and combine well, then season to taste with salt and pepper.

Line a pie tin with pâte brisée (see instructions on page 52), fill with the pumpkin filling and cover with puff pastry (see instructions on page 12).

Score the pastry surface, brush with a drizzle of oil and dust with sesame and sunflower seeds. Bake at 190°C/375°F/ Gas 5 for 30 minutes and serve warm.

### PUFF PASTRY

To prepare a workmanlike pastry, it's very important that all the ingredients are at the same temperature; margarine in particular must have the same temperature as pastry (can't be substituted with butter).

# Browned roll with vegetables and mushrooms

**Serves 4**

### Roll

250g/9oz filo pastry
1 bunch of medium asparagus
3 carrots
2 medium-small porcini mushrooms
6 tbsp extra virgin olive oil
2 cloves of garlic, crushed
thyme, torn
salt and pepper

### Salad

2 Caesar's mushrooms (*Amanita Caesarea*)
3 tbsp extra virgin olive oil
salt and pepper

**Preparation time:** 25 minutes
**Cooking time:** 15 minutes
**Difficulty:** easy
**Wine:** Trentino Sylvaner

Cut away the hard bottom of the asparagus stalks and steam until just done.

Peel the carrots, cut them into julienne strips and steam for 3 minutes.

Wipe the mushrooms with damp kitchen paper towels and discard the earthy bottom of the stems; dice them and cook in a pan with oil and garlic. Add salt and pepper and flavour with the thyme.

Roll out the filo pastry in two overlapping layers, salt and arrange the asparagus in parallel lines (1cm/½in from each other). Fill in the spaces with carrots then salt. Season with a drizzle of oil and sprinkle with mushrooms. Slowly roll up the pastry and brush with oil, and salt.

Bake at 220°C/425°F/Gas 7 for 10 minutes. Serve the roll on a Caesar's mushrooms salad seasoned with salt, oil and pepper.

# Salmon strudel with broad bean and balsamic sauce

## Serves 4

### *Strudel*
350g/12oz puff pastry
200g/7oz/1 cup fresh salmon flesh
4 tbsp extra virgin olive oil
butter
chives
lemon thyme
salt

### *Bean sauce*
100g/3½oz/1 cup broad beans, shelled
100ml/3½fl oz/½ cup fresh single cream
60g/2¼oz/¼ cup butter
1 shallot, cut into julienne strips
½ chilli, chopped

### *To garnish*
puff pastry trimmings
oil for deep-frying
balsamic vinegar

**Preparation time:** 25 minutes
**Cooking time:** 30 minutes
**Difficulty:** medium
**Wine:** Friuli Isonzo Chardonnay

Chop the salmon flesh adding extra virgin olive oil, salt and aromatic herbs, then arrange the mixture on the pastry (see instructions on page 12). Slowly roll up, brush with a little melted butter and score the surface with a series of diagonal incisions.

Meanwhile, cook the shallot in butter with the chilli; blanch the beans and cook in a saucepan with the shallot. Pour in little warm water and before cooking is completed add the cream. Process the mixture in a food processor and pass through a sieve.

Place the strudel on greaseproof paper and bake at 190°C/375F°/Gas 5 for 20 minutes. Leave to cool slightly then slice into 4 portions.

Deep-fry the puff pastry trimmings. Serve salmon strudel on cold cream together with balsamic vinegar and puff pastry trimmings.

# Pie filled with chicken and artichoke hearts

**Serves 6**

### Pastry
200g/7oz/1 cup plain white flour
1 tsp yeast for savoury pies
3 tbsp extra virgin olive oil
salt and pepper

### Stuffing
300g/11oz chicken breast
5 globe artichokes
3 tbsp extra virgin olive oil
1 shallot, chopped
1 egg
2-3 tbsp fresh single cream
1 tbsp Parmesan cheese, grated
1 lemon
parsley or chives, chopped
salt and pepper

**Preparation time:** 25 minutes
**Cooking time:** 35 minutes
**Difficulty:** easy
**Wine:** Bardolino Chiaretto

Sift the flour in a bowl with yeast, salt and pepper. Pour in the oil and little lukewarm water. Knead on a floured surface until the dough ball is elastic and smooth; wrap in clingfilm and allow to rest.

Discard the artichoke outer leaves, cut away the hard part of the stalks and leave the hearts in water acidulated with 1 tbsp lemon juice.

Cut the chicken breast into small pieces and quickly brown the shallot in oil. Blend in the sliced artichoke hearts, season with salt and pepper and flavour with parsley. Cook until just done, then add the chicken and cook for 3 more minutes.

Beat the egg in a bowl with the cream, add both Parmesan cheese and the tepid chicken mixture. Roll out the pastry flattening it with a rolling pin, line a round mould with high rims. Prick the base with a fork and fill with the chicken-artichoke mixture.

Cover the surface with pastry trimmings, leaving just a small hole in the middle for the steam to escape. Bake at 200°C/400°F/Gas 6 for about 18-20 minutes and serve.

# Potato and bacon pie with puff pastry

**Serves 6**

### *Pastry*

400g/14oz/2 cups potatoes, peeled and cut into round slices
250g/9oz puff pastry
1 shallot, chopped
500ml/18fl oz/2¼ cups vegetable stock
80g/2¾oz bacon, diced
1 egg
3 tbsp Parmesan cheese, grated
2 tbsp extra virgin olive oil
1 tbsp sesame seeds
salt and pepper

**Preparation time:** 20 minutes
**Cooking time:** 45 minutes
**Difficulty:** easy
**Wine:** Prosecco di Conegliano
e Valdobbiadene Extra Dry

Brown the shallot in a pan with oil. Add the potatoes and sauté; pour in the hot stock (see photo 1) and cook over medium-low heat until they are tender. Purée the potatoes with a hand blender, then season to taste with salt and pepper.

Put the bacon in a non-stick pan adding a drizzle of oil to make it crispy. Combine bacon and potatoes (see photo 2), then add the beaten egg (see photo 3), the cheese and a little pepper.

Line a pyrex dish with greaseproof paper, fill it with the mixture and cover with the pricked puff pastry (see instructions on page 12). Dust with sesame seeds and bake at 200°C/400°F/Gas 6 for about 35 minutes. Leave to cool slightly then serve.

# Courgette, bacon and caprino cheese (Italian goats cheese) flan

**Serves 4**

### *Pâte brisée*
200g/7oz/1 cup plain white flour
100g/3½oz/½ cup butter
1 tbsp extra virgin olive oil
1 egg
salt

### *Stuffing*
400g/14oz/2 cups courgettes, diced
100g/3½oz/½ cup bacon, finely chopped
30g/1oz/2 tbsp pine nuts
100g/3½oz/½ cup fresh caprino cheese, diced
3 tbsp extra virgin olive oil
2 tbsp Parmesan cheese, grated
4 eggs
200ml/7fl oz/1 cup milk
100ml/3½fl oz/½ cup fresh single cream
2 cloves of garlic, crushed
salt and pepper

**Preparation time:** 20 minutes
**Cooking time:** 40 minutes
**Difficulty:** medium
**Wine:** Friuli Pinot Grigio

Prepare the pâte brisée (see instructions on page 52), wrap it in clingfilm and allow to rest in a cool place for 20 minutes. Sauté the courgettes in a saucepan with garlic cloves and olive oil. Brown them quickly until tender. Season to taste with salt and pepper and leave to cool slightly.

In a bowl beat the eggs with Parmesan cheese, milk, cream and bacon. Add salt and pepper.

Remove the garlic cloves and process the courgettes with a food processor; towards the end add the caprino cheese then process for a few more seconds. Combine with the egg mixture and mix well.

Roll out the pâte brisée until thin and line a mould (24 cm/9½ in in diameter). Stuff the base with the courgette-egg mixture, blanch the pine nuts and sprinkle them on the top; cut away the excess edges. Bake at 160°C/325°F/Gas 3 for 25-30 minutes and serve the pie cut into slices.

# Millet pie with pumpkin and mushrooms

### Serves 4

### *Pie*
200g/7oz/1 cup millet
350g/12oz/1½ cup pumpkin
1 tbsp dried mushrooms
1 shallot, chopped
1 bunch of parsley, chopped
2 tbsp soya sauce
5 tbsp breadcrumbs
2 tbsp extra virgin olive oil
salt

### *Bechamel*
2 tbsp plain white flour
3 tbsp corn oil
300ml/10fl oz/1¼ cups soya milk

**Preparation time:** 30 minutes
**Cooking time:** 30 minutes
**Difficulty:** easy
**Wine:** Alto Adige Sauvignon

Soak the dried mushrooms in lukewarm water. Peel the pumpkin and thinly slice it; wash the millet in a fine-mesh strainer and put it in a saucepan with the pumpkin and a pinch of salt. Pour in 400ml/14fl oz/1½ cups water, cover and leave to cook over low heat for 20 minutes. Turn off and allow to rest for 10 minutes.

Brown the shallot quickly in a pan with olive oil; press and coarsely chop mushrooms and add to shallot. Season with salt, pour in 100ml/3½fl oz/½ cup of water and cook gently for 10 minutes.

Heat the corn oil in a saucepan, put in the flour and leave to cook for 2-3 minutes. Pour in the soya milk gradually and cook stirring constantly for 10-15 minutes.

Combine mushrooms, chopped parsley and soya sauce with the millet. Stir well and spread the mixture in a baking tin (20cm/8 in in diameter) greased and dusted with breadcrumbs. Level off the surface and spread over the bechamel. Dust with breadcrumbs and bake at 180°C/350F°/Gas 4 for 25 minutes.

# Pumpkin pie with leek and tofu sauce

### Serves 4

### *Pie*
½ Mantuan pumpkin (*Cucurbita maxima*), skin removed and sliced
250g/9oz/1 cup plain white flour
120ml/4fl oz/½ cup water
½ block of Brewer's yeast
2 tbsp sunflower oil

### *Sauce*
200g/7oz/1 cup tofu, crumbled
1 leek, chopped
1 tbsp extra virgin olive oil

**Preparation time:** 30 minutes
**Cooking time:** 75 minutes
**Difficulty:** easy
**Wine:** Ribolla Gialla

Bake the pumpkin slices at 180°C/350°F/Gas 4 for 20 minutes. Weigh 250g/9oz/1 cup of baked pumpkin. Meanwhile, dissolve the Brewer's yeast in lukewarm water, adding sunflower oil.

Chop the pumkin flesh in a mixer and addit to the flour; quickly work all the ingredients. Leave to rest for 1 hour. Knead it again, stretch it with little flour until 1cm/½ in thick, using a rolling pin. Allow to rest for 30 more minutes, then bake at 160°C/325°F/Gas 3 for 40 minutes.

Meanwhile, cook the leek in a saucepan with 1 tablespoon of oil. As soon as it becomes transparent, add the tofu and cook over low heat for 10 minutes.

Remove the pie from the oven and leave to cool slightly on a metal. Slice in half horizontally. Spread with the tofu sauce and bake for 5 more minutes. Serve warm.

**Note -** Leek has many healthy properties. It contains vitamin C and B, iron, calcium, phosphorus, magnesium, potassium, manganese and other minerals. Like garlic and onion, leek strengthens the immune system and has an antioxidant function.

# Spinach and fresh ricotta pie

**Serves 4**

### *Pie*

350g/12oz puff pastry
1 bunch of spinach and Swiss chard (about 350g/12oz/1½ cups cooked)
200g/7oz/1 cup fresh ricotta cheese
3 tbsp Parmesan cheese, grated
1 egg
3 tbsp extra virgin olive oil
nutmeg
salt and pepper

**Preparation time:** 25 minutes
**Cooking time:** 45 minutes
**Difficulty:** easy
**Wine:** Müller Thurgau

Thoroughly wash the spinach and the Swiss chard in cold water, turning them over in a bowl.

Remove the root from the spinach and the hard white part from the chard. Wash them again and simmer in salted water for about 5 minutes. Drain and leave to cool. Chop them with a cook's knife. Blend in the egg, the Parmesan cheese and the nutmeg; season to taste with salt and pepper. Combine with ricotta cheese and olive oil; add salt if necessary and set aside.

Roll out the puff pastry (see instructions on page 12) on a floured surface, sprinkle some flour in a round mould (20 cm/8in in diameter) then line it with pastry leaving some overlapping. Prick the base with a fork and fill with the stuffing. Fold the excess edges of the pastry towards the middle and bake at 190°C/375°F/Gas 5 for approximately 25 minutes. Remove the pie from the oven and leave to cool; place on a plate and serve.

# Rustic pie with tuna and broccoli

## Serves 6

### Pie

300g/11oz pâte brisée
200g/7oz/1 cup tuna in oil, drained
4 slices of sandwich loaf
200ml/6fl oz/1 cup of milk
2 tbsp capers
1 red onion, peeled and thinly sliced
1 broccoli top
3 tbsp extra virgin olive oil
1 clove of garlic, crushed
½ red chilli, seeded and chopped
parsley
salt and pepper

**Preparation time:** 20 minutes
**Cooking time:** 40 minutes
**Difficulty:** easy
**Wine:** Bianco d'Alcamo

Cut the bread into small pieces and soak in a bowl of cold milk.

Wash the broccoli and pick off the florets; blanch them in salted water for 3 minutes, drain and stir-fry with oil, garlic and chilli. Cook on a high heat and salt slightly. When ready, place in a bowl.

Put tuna, capers, lightly pressed bread and parsley in a mixer, then process. Combine the obtained mixture with broccoli and season to taste with salt and pepper.

Roll out the pastry (see instructions on page 52) on a floured surface. Flour a round aluminium mould and line it with the pastry. Prick the base with a fork and fill with the mixture.

Sprinkle the onion on top of the pie. Season with a drizzle of olive oil and bake at 200°C/400°F/Gas 6 for 30-35 minutes.

### TUNA IN OIL

Tuna in oil is certainly one of the most popular fish products in the world, that's why there are many different qualities. Obviously the best products are those made with fresh tuna.
If tuna is available in a tin, it would be better, once opened, to decant to a jar to avoid altering the tuna characteristics.

# Pumpkin, carrot and courgette flan

**Serves 6-8**

### *Flan*
400g/14oz pâte brisée
¼ round, green-skinned pumpkin
3 courgettes
1 white onion, finely chopped
2 tbsp butter
2 tbsp extra virgin olive oil
2 carrots, peeled and diced
1 egg
50g/1¾oz/¼ cup pumpkin seeds
500ml/18fl oz/2¼ cups vegetable stock
thyme, chopped
salt and pepper

**Preparation time:** 25 minutes
**Cooking time:** 50 minutes
**Difficulty:** easy
**Wine:** Gambellara

Wash the courgettes and cut away their tips; slice into 4 pieces lengthwise and discard the white heart with its seeds. Dice and set aside.

Peel the pumpkin on a chopping board using a serrated-edge knife, remove the seeds and the stringy parts, then dice.

Cook the onion in a saucepan with the oil and butter, add the carrots and shortly afterwards the pumpkin. Sauté adding a little salt and pepper. Pour in the hot stock, cover and cook for 7 minutes. Add the courgettes and finish cooking.

Leave to cool. Roll out the pâte brisée (instructions on page 52) on a floured surface to 4 mm/¼in thick.
Flour a round flan mould with it, line the pastry and prick the base with a fork.

Combine egg and thyme with the vegetable stuffing and fill the mould levelling off the top. Sprinkle with pumpkin seeds and bake at 190°C/375°F/Gas 5 for about 40 minutes.

# Sesame pie with aubergine sauce

**Serves 6**

### *Pastry*
220g/7½oz/1 cup plain white flour
1 tbsp sesame oil
2 tbsp sesame seeds
½ tsp yeast
salt

### *Sauce*
1 large aubergine (or 2 small)
4 large courgettes
2 spring onions, chopped
3 tbsp extra virgin olive oil
1 egg white
2 tbsp Parmesan cheese, grated
100ml/3½fl oz/½ cup vegetable stock or water
lemon thyme, torn
salt and pepper

**Preparation time:** 20 minutes
**Cooking time:** 50 minutes
**Difficulty:** easy
**Wine:** Friuli Collio Sauvignon

Toast the sesame seeds in a non-stick pan until nicely browned. Pour the flour into a bowl, then add the yeast, the salt, the sesame oil and the sesame seeds. Pour in little lukewarm water and knead. Wrap the pastry in clingfilm and leave to rest in the fridge.

Cut the aubergine into 8 segments, discarding the white heart with seeds. Cut the courgettes into thin round slices and dice the aubergine. Brown the spring onions in a saucepan with oil over low heat and blend in the aubergine. Cover and cook for 5-6 minutes, adding a pinch of salt.

Add the courgettes, sauté together with thyme and pour in the warm stock. Cook until vegetables are tender, then process in a food mixer. Leave to cool slightly, then add the egg white partially beaten with a little salt and cheese. Season to taste with salt and pepper.

Roll out the pastry and line a floured mould; prick the base with a fork and fill with the vegetable sauce. Bake at 200°C/400°F/Gas 6 for 35 minutes. Serve at room temperature or cold.

# Pastry purses filled with salmon trout

**Serves 4**

### Pastry
500g/1lb 2oz/3¼ cups plain white flour
8 tbsp extra virgin olive oil
150ml/5fl oz/½ cup water
salt

### Filling
300g/11oz fillet of salmon trout
250g/9oz/1 cup cauliflower
200g/7oz/1 cup Savoy cabbage, thinly sliced
6 tbsp extra virgin olive oil
50ml/2fl oz/¼ cup white wine
1 egg
1 shallot, chopped
1 sprig of parsley, chopped
1 clove of garlic, crushed
salt and white pepper

**Preparation time:** 40 minutes
**Cooking time:** 30 minutes
**Difficulty:** medium
**Wine:** Terlaner

Work the flour with oil, water and a pinch of salt until the dough becomes elastic: wrap it in clingfilm and allow to rest in the fridge.

Cut away the cauliflower florets and blanch them in hot salted water and wine for 5 minutes; drain and leave to cool in a bowl with cold water and ice. Wash the Savoy cabbage, stir-fry with oil and garlic, season with salt and pepper then set aside.

Discard the fillet skin and bones, then dice it; gently cook the shallot in a saucepan with little water and a sprig of parsley.

Preheat the oven to 200°C/400°F/Gas 6. Flatten the pastry until 0.5cm/¼in thick using a rolling pin. Cut the pastry into 5cm/2in squares; place a teaspoon of Savoy cabbage, some piece of salmon trout and 1 cauliflower florets onto the middle of each square.

Complete with a teaspoon of the shallot and close to make a purse. Brush with beaten egg and bake for 20 minutes. Serve hot.

# Focaccias

Thin and crispy flat breads enriched
with simple and tasty ingredients.
Easy and quick recipes
to prepare light and original meals
or to accompany an
appetizer with friends.

# Focaccia with onions and black olives

**Serves 4**

### Dough
500g/1lb 2oz/3¼ cups plain white flour
1½ tbsp Brewer's yeast
½ tsp honey
2 tbsp extra virgin olive oil
salt

### Topping
3 medium onions, sliced
2 tbsp black olives, stoned
2 tbsp extra virgin olive oil
marjoram and oregano

**Preparation time:** 15 minutes
**Cooking time:** 35 minutes
**Difficulty:** easy
**Wine:** Alto Adige Pinot Grigio

Dissolve the yeast in lukewarm water with ½ teaspoon of honey; allow to rest for about 10 minutes.

Prepare the focaccia dough mixing flour with salt, oil and yeast. Leave to rest for 3 hours.

Quickly brown the onions with 2 tablespoons of oil and 2 tablespoons of water until transparent. Add olives, oregano and marjoram.

Stretch or roll the dough on an oiled baking tin, sprinkle with onions and olives and bake at 150°C/300°F/Gas 2 for 25 minutes. Serve hot.

**Tip -** If you don't like the strong smell of onions, slice them into rings and try to bake in a microwave oven at maximum power for 1 minute. In this way, their pungent aroma will partially evaporate.

**ONION**
5000 years ago onion was already cultivated in some areas of North Asia and in Palestine; moreover, as some documents attest, it was much appreciated by both Egyptians and Greeks (at the time of Peloponnesian wars, onion was the army food par excellence).

# Sweetcorn focaccia with bacon

**Serves 4**

### *Focaccia*
300g/11oz focaccia dough
50g/1¾oz/¼ cup corn meal
150g/5oz streaky bacon, diced
3 tbsp extra virgin olive oil
1 bunch of aromatic herbs (rosemary, sage, thyme, chives), chopped
salt and pepper

**Preparation time:** 20 minutes
**Cooking time:** 25 minutes
**Difficulty:** easy
**Wine:** Lambrusco di Sorbara

Let the dough rise well (see instructions on page 10), then knead thoroughly adding 2 tablespoons of bacon and a sprinkle of corn meal.

Roll out the dough on a baking tray, leaving it rather thick. Brush with extra virgin olive oil and dust with corn meal. Fill a vaporizer with water and spray the focaccia at a distance of 30cm/12in, so to dampen its surface. Lightly season with salt and pepper and leave to rise in a warm place for about 20 minutes.

Bake at 200°C/400°F/Gas 6 for 25 minutes; halfway through the cooking add the aromatic herbs and the remaining bacon, so that its fat melts on the focaccia surface. Remove from the oven, cut into slices and, if you like, serve with boiled vegetables.

# Schiacciata with tomatoes and oregano

**Serves 4**

### *Schiacciata*
400g/14oz focaccia dough
2 red tomatoes
1 tsp oregano
4 tbsp extra virgin olive oil
salt and pepper

**Preparation time:** 10 minutes
**Cooking time:** 20 minutes
**Difficulty:** easy
**Wine:** Vermentino della Riviera Ligure
di Ponente

Work the dough (see instructions on page 10) rolling it on a floured surface, then line a lightly oiled baking tray. Dust the dough with a little salt and pepper, brush with oil and leave to rise in a warm place for 25 minutes.

Meanwhile, wash the tomatoes and cut them using a serrated knife. Arrange them on the focaccia leaving 1cm/ ½in space between the slices; dust with oregano and a pinch of salt.

Bake at 230°C/450°F/Gas 8 for about 20 minutes. Leave to cool slightly, then cut into slices and serve as a tasty afternoon snack.

**Cook's tip -** If you prefer a tastier focaccia, you can use dried San Marzano tomatoes marinaded in oil (easily available in any supermarket). In this way, the tomatoes will have a much richer flavour.

# Puff pastry crackers with rosemary

**Serves 4-6**

### Crackers
150g/5oz/1 cup plain white flour
4 tbsp sunflower oil
2 tbsp extra virgin olive oil
2 sprigs of rosemary
salt flakes

**Preparation time:** 10 minutes
**Cooking time:** 4 minutes
**Difficulty:** easy
**Wine:** Elba Bianco

Pour the flour into a bowl, add sunflower oil, extra virgin olive oil and the chopped leaves of rosemary. Pour in a little lukewarm water (about 4 tablespoons) and knead with your fingertips to make a smooth dough.

Place the dough on a worktop and knead energically with the palm of your hands, adding some flour if the dough looks too soft and wet. Work unitl you get a smooth and elastic ball, wrap it in clingfilm and allow to rest in the fridge for about 20 minutes.

Cut the dough into strips and flatten them, a piece at a time, using a pasta maker (you can also use a rolling pin, taking care to flour the worktop after each roll).
As soon as the strips are thin enough, arrange them in a baking tray; dust with the remaining rosemary and salt. Bake at 250°C/480°F/Gas 9 for about 4 minutes, then leave to cool.

**Cook's tip -** If you break the pasta strips into pieces, you'll get small and tasty crackers, which are great to accompany a meal or to eat as a snack.

## SUNFLOWER OIL
If not used for frying, sunflower oil is suited for those recipes that require an oil with a slight taste. Alternatively you can choose a very delicate extra virgin olive oil.

# Focaccia with green olives and peppers

**Serves 4**

### *Focaccia*

350g/12oz focaccia dough
20 green olives, stoned
1 red pepper
3 tbsp extra virgin olive oil
1 clove garlic
salt

**Preparation time:** 20 minutes
**Cooking time:** 30 minutes
**Difficulty:** easy
**Wine:** Trentino Nosiola

Wash the red pepper, cut it in half, remove the white inner pith and the seeds. Cut into small strips and set aside.

Drain the olives and dry them on kitchen paper towels.

Roll out the well-risen dough (see instructions on page 10), line an oiled baking tray and arrange the olives on the focaccia. Leave to rise again in a warm place for 20 minutes.

Meanwhile, peel the garlic and brown it quickly in a saucepan with oil; add the peppers and cook on high for about 7-8 minutes.

Drain the excess oil and sprinkle the peppers on the focaccia. Add a pinch of salt and bake at 220°C/425°F/Gas 7 for about 18 minutes.

Take out of the oven, remove the focaccia from the baking tray and cut it into rectangular slices.

**Tip -** To fasten and simplify the preparation of this focaccia, you can use raw peppers; thinly slice them, season with salt, pepper, olive oil and thyme, then bake them with the dough.

# Focaccia with white onions, anchovies and capers

**Serves 4**

### *Focaccia*
350g/12oz focaccia dough
2 small white onions
10 anchovy fillets, in oil
1 tbsp capers, drained and rinsed
3 tbsp extra virgin olive oil
salt and pepper

**Preparation time:** 20 minutes
**Cooking time:** 18 minutes
**Difficulty:** easy
**Wine:** Bianco d'Alcamo

Peel the onions and thinly slice them into rings; put in a bowl with cold water so that they lose their strong flavour. Drain the anchovy fillets and coarsely chop them.

Thoroughly wash the capers and lightly chop using a knife or a crescent-shaped mincing knife.

Grease a baking tray and line it with the dough (see instructions on page 10), stretching it first with a rolling pin then using your fingertips.

Drain the onions, dry them with kitchen paper towels and spread over the focaccia. Leave to rise in a warm place for about 20 minutes (under a damp cloth).

Sprinkle with chopped capers, anchovy fillets and the remaining oil, then bake at 220°C/425°F/Gas 7 for 18 minutes.

Leave to cool, season to taste, cut the focaccia into small pieces and serve.

# Saffron yellow focaccia in a courgette crust

**Serves 4**

### Focaccia
300g/11oz focaccia dough
1 sachet of saffron
3 courgettes "Long of Florence"
3 tbsp extra virgin olive oil
salt and black pepper

**Preparation time:** 20 minutes
**Cooking time:** 15 minutes
**Difficulty:** easy
**Wine:** Elba Bianco

Stir a sachet of saffron with 1 tbsp of water and add it to the dough. Stretch or roll the dough until thin (see instructions on page 10), lay it into a lightly oiled baking tray and leave to rest and rise in a warm place.

Meanwhile, wash the courgettes and cut away their tips; cut them into thin round slices using a mandoline slicer or a sharp knife.

Brush the dough surface with oil, add salt and arrange the courgettes lightly overlapping. Add some more salt and pepper.

Bake at 220°C/425°F/Gas 7 for about 17-18 minutes, until the edges are nicely browned. Leave to cool, cut into squares and serve.

**Cook's tip -** You can mix some saffron pistils with the dough, so that you can see them in the slices, and flavour the dough with thyme to make it even more savoury and special.

# Savoury focaccia with apples

**Serves 6**

### *Focaccia*
450g/1lb/3 cups plain white flour
1½ tbsp Brewer's yeast
200ml/7fl oz/1 cup water
1 apple, diced
25g/1oz/1½ tbsp shallot
1 tsp marjoram
1 tsp icing sugar
3 tbsp extra virgin olive oil
a pinch of salt

**Preparation time:** 15 minutes
**Cooking time:** 40 minutes
**Difficulty:** easy
**Wine:** Alto Adige Gewürztraminer

Mix the flour with the water, yeast and salt. Work the dough energically and then allow to rest for about 15 minutes.

Cook the apple in oil together with shallot, icing sugar and marjoram. Combine this mixture with the dough and leave to rest for 2 hours, until it doubles in volume.

Roll out the dough and bake in a preheated oven at 185°C/365°F/Gas 5 for 17 minutes, then reduce the temperature to 150°C/300°F/Gas 2 and continue cooking for another 13 minutes.

Serve the focaccia warm together with different cuts of cold meats.

# More than sandwiches

Piadinas, cannoli and panzerotti
to whet your appetite.
Recipes for all tastes, which can turn
a quick lunch or
a simple snack with friends
into a moment of real pleasure.

# Fried "nuvolette" with asparagus

**Serves 4**

### Nuvolette
200g/7oz panzerotti dough
6 thin asparagus
oil for deep-frying
1 sprig of thyme
salt and ground black pepper

**Preparation time:** 10 minutes
**Cooking time:** 10 minutes
**Difficulty:** easy
**Wine:** Colli di Conegliano Verdiso

Slightly peel the asparagus using a peeler and discard the hard bottom of the stalks. Blanch them in boiling salted water (for about 3 minutes), drain and dip in cold water, then cut into thin round slices.

Work the dough (see instructions on page 13) with a pinch of ground black pepper, thyme and thinly sliced asparagus; combine all the ingredients well.

Heat the oil and deep-fry spoonfuls of dough. Drain on kitchen paper towels, add salt and serve immediately.

**Tip -** If you prefer lighter croquettes, instead of the classic panzerotti dough, you can use a rather thick batter, made with flour and cold sparkling water, mixed with asparagus and thyme.

# Rustic sandwiches with crescenza cheese and finocchiona

**Serves 4**

### Sandwiches

4 thick slices of rustic bread (e.g. Altamura)
130g/4½oz/1 cup fresh crescenza or stracchino cheese
150g/5oz finocchiona, sliced
1 tbsp extra virgin olive oil
black pepper

**Preparation time:** 10 minutes
**Difficulty:** easy
**Wine:** Morellino di Scansano

Stir the crescenza with extra virgin olive oil until creamy and smooth, spread it on the bread slices. Dust with black pepper and cover two slices with the finocchiona. Cover with the remaining two slices and gently press down.

Cut the sandwiches into two halves and serve with a glass of good red wine.

**Note -** Finocchiona is a crumbly salami, that's why it is also called "sbriciolona" in Tuscany. This salami contains fennel seeds which give it its particular taste and, at the same time, improve its long preservation. Fennel was used for this purpose especially in the past, when pepper was rare and expensive.

**ALTAMURA BREAD**
It's a typical Apulian product, naturally leavened and baked in wood-fired ovens. It is well-known and appreciated for its numerous qualities: crispy crust and soft crumbs, wholesomeness and long life.

# Crispy piadina with crab salad

**Serves 4**

### *Piadinas*

4 small-medium piadinas
1 head of green salad (gentilina or iceberg)
1 tin of natural crab pulp (about 200g/7oz/1 cup)
150g/5oz/1 cup grilled aubergines in oil
10 cherry tomatoes
3 tbsp extra virgin olive oil
½ lemon
parsley, chopped
salt and pepper

**Preparation time:** 20 minutes
**Cooking time:** 10 minutes
**Difficulty:** easy
**Wine:** Trebbiano di Romagna

Thoroughly wash the salad in cold water and dry it in a salad spinner; wash tomatoes too.

Drain the crab pulp and season it with oil, salt, pepper and parsley. Add the lemon juice and pour this mixture on the finely sliced salad.

Cut the tomatoes into 4 segments, drain aubergines and wipe them with kitchen paper towels.

Place the piadinas in a preheated oven at 180°C/350°F/ Gas 4 for 7 minutes, until crispy. If necessary, season the salad with salt and oil, and mix all the ingredients thoroughly. Serve the salad arranged on the 4 crunchy piadinas.

# Calabrese stringy purses

## Serves 4

### Stringy purses

220g/7½oz panzerotto dough
150g/5oz/1 cup mozzarella cheese
1 tbsp capers, drained and rinsed
100g/3½oz/1 cup dried San Marzano tomatoes
oil for deep-frying
oregano
salt

**Preparation time:** 15 minutes
**Cooking time:** 5 minutes
**Difficulty:** easy
**Wine:** Cirò Bianco

Soak the tomatoes in a little lukewarm water for about
1 hour. Drain and dry them, then coarsely chop using a knife.

Dice the mozzarella cheese and keep it in the fridge.
Thoroughly wash the capers, changing the water three times,
drain and chop. Put the three ingredients in a bowl
and season with oregano.

Roll out the pastry (see instructions on page 13) on a floured
surface and cut it into small squares. Place some filling
in the middle of each square, fold and seal the edges
pressing gently with your fingertips.

Deep-fry the pastry purses in hot oil and drain them
on kitchen paper towels; add salt and serve immediately.

**Tip -** If you prefer a tastier mixture, you can use dried
tomatoes marinated in a mixture of olive oil, garlic, chilli
and oregano. As soon as you open the panzerotto in your
hands, it will give off an intense and pervading smell. Melting
mozzarella will become stringy and contrast with the strong
taste of tomatoes and capers.

# Piadina with buffalo mozzarella, grilled tomatoes, prosciutto and basil

**Serves 4**

### *Piadinas*
4 piadinas
3 red tomatoes
100g/3½oz prosciutto, thinly sliced
300g/11oz/1½ cup buffalo mozzarella, thinly sliced
1 bunch of fresh basil
a pinch of oregano
2 tbsp extra virgin olive oil
salt

**Preparation time:** 15 minutes
**Cooking time:** 5 minutes
**Difficulty:** easy
**Wine:** Tocai Friulano

Wash the tomatoes and cut them into thick slices. Heat a ridged grill pan and grill them 1 minute per side; add salt and dust with oregano.

Fill the warm piadinas with mozzarella cheese, prosciutto and tomato slices, alternating and slightly overlapping.

Season with salt and olive oil, then wash and dry the basil leaves. Fold over the piadinas and serve immediately.

**Note -** The contrast between warm grilled tomatoes and fresh mozzarella leaves a pleasant contrast in the palate and gives to piadina a very particular taste.

### PROSCIUTTO
This is a typical Italian product and it comes in a wide variety, the most famous are Parma, San Daniele and Norcia. The differences in taste mainly depend on the microclimate in which they are left to mature. This is the reason why each kind of prosciutto is produced exclusively in particular and limited areas.

# Cannolo with ricotta cheese and olive paste

**Serves 4**

### Cannolo
4 thin and soft piadinas
250g/9oz/1 cup fresh ricotta cheese
120g/4oz/1 cup black olives, stoned (or olive paste)
1 sprig of thyme, chopped
3 San Marzano tomatoes
2 tbsp extra virgin olive oil
salt and pepper

### To garnish
1 bunch of rocket
black olives

**Preparation time:** 15 minutes
**Difficulty:** easy
**Wine:** Valcalepio Bianco

Put the ricotta cheese and the olives in a food mixer, add a pinch of salt and process until you get a dark grey, smooth and tasty paste (if you use olive paste, simply combine it with the ricotta cheese in a bowl).

Wash the tomatoes, dry and cut them into 4 segments. Remove the seeds and thinly dice the pulp. Season with thyme, salt, pepper and a drizzle of oil. Leave to marinate, then drain.

Spread the olive paste on piadinas leaving 2cm/¾in round the edges and sprinkle with diced tomatoes. Roll in the shape of a horn (cannolo) and leave to rest for 10 minutes. Cut into small pieces and serve cold on a bed of rocket and the oil of black olives.

# Mini croquettes with stuffed olives

**Serves 4**

### *Croquettes*
180g/6½oz panzerotto dough
2 tbsp corn meal
20 green olives stuffed with red pepper
oil for deep-frying
salt

**Preparation time:** 10 minutes
**Cooking time:** 5 minutes
**Difficulty:** easy
**Wine:** Ortrugo Frizzante

On a floured surface knead the dough (see instructions on page 13) with the corn meal to make it as thin as possible. Drain the olives and dry them on a tray covered with several sheets of kitchen paper towels.

Cut the dough into strips 3cm/¼in wide and 5cm/2in long. Arrange the olives at the front end of each strip, roll up and seal the edges pressing gently with your fingertips.

Heat the oil in a saucepan and fry the mini croquettes. Drain well on kitchen paper towels, add a pinch of salt and serve.

**Note -** By sprinkling a bit of corn meal on the outside of the dough, you'll have a much crispier croquette. Mini croquettes are particularly suited as appetizers with a good glass of wine or before hors d'oeuvre at a dinner with guests.

# Mini pizzas with peppers and mushrooms

**Serves 4**

### *Pizzas*

250g/9oz puff pastry
½ red pepper
½ yellow pepper
½ green pepper
2 mushrooms
3 tbsp extra virgin olive oil
thyme, torn
salt and pepper

**Preparation time:** 20 minutes
**Cooking time:** 20 minutes
**Difficulty:** easy
**Wine:** Prosecco di Valdobbiadene Brut

Wash the peppers and finely dice them (see photo 1). Thoroughly skin the mushrooms using a sharp knife, discard the earthy bottom of the stems and thinly slice them.

Heat the oil in a frying pan and sauté the peppers, put in the mushrooms and cook further for few minutes (see photo 2). Season to taste with salt and pepper.

Roll out the puff pastry and cut it using a round pasta cutter. Place the pepper-mushroom mixture in the middle (see photo 3). Dust with thyme and bake at 200°C/400°F/Gas 6 for about 15 minutes. Serve warm as hors d'oeuvre or as a tasty appetizer.

1    2    3

# Sandwiches with bresaola, tomatoes and Parmesan cheese

**Serves 4**

### *Sandwiches*
4 wholemeal rolls
12 slices of bresaola
10 cherry tomatoes
3 tbsp Parmesan cheese
extra virgin olive oil
salt

**Preparation time:** 5 minutes
**Difficulty:** easy
**Wine:** Valcalepio Bianco

Wash and cut the cherry tomatoes in half; season them with a drizzle of extra virgin olive oil and a pinch of salt and set aside.

Cut some thin flakes from the Parmesan cheese using a peeler; cut the wholemeal rolls lengthwise and fill each sandwich with 4 slices of bresaola, tomatoes and Parmesan flakes.

Close the rolls and, if you like, serve with some lettuce leaves.

**Tip -** If you prefer, you can use 4 slices of Parma ham instead of bresaola and the same amount of half-aged pecorino cheese instead of Parmesan.

# Bread

Rolls, loaves and breadsticks
to bring the fragrance
of the best bakeries
directly into your kitchens.
Recipes, never banal,
to surprise and make the simplest of
food the protagonist at the table.

# Mediterranean bread

## Ingredients
(700g/1lb 9oz bread)

### 1st dough
250g/9oz/1 cup plain white flour
135ml/4½fl oz/½ cup water
½ tbsp Brewer's yeast

### 2nd dough
250g/9oz/1 cup plain white flour
135ml/4½fl oz/½ cup water
3 tbsp extra virgin olive oil
a pinch of salt

**Preparation time:** 40 minutes
**Cooking time:** 30 minutes
**Difficulty:** difficult

Prepare the first dough mixing flour, lukewarm water and yeast. Leave to rise at room temperature under a cloth for about 3 hours.

Then combine with the flour required for the second dough, 100ml/3½fl oz/½ cup lukewarm water and the extra virgin olive oil. Mix the salt with the remaining water, pour it gently over the dough and go on kneading. Place the dough in a slightly oiled bowl and leave to rise for about 20 minutes. Stretch or roll the dough on a worktop and oil it; fold it up 4 times and allow to rest for 20 minutes.

Divide the dough and shape it into rolls (see photos 1-2-3). Arrange them on an oven-proof plate, brush with olive oil and dust generously with flour. After 10 minutes, place the rolls on baking trays and let rise at room temperature for 60 minutes, sheltered from draughts.

Bake at 240°C/475°F/Gas 9 until the rolls are nicely browned.

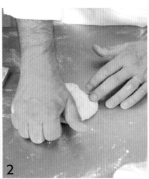
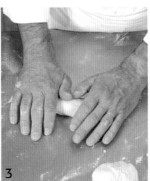

# Large malt breadsticks

**Ingredients** (35 breadsticks)

### 1st dough

150g/5oz/1 cup semolina
100ml/3½fl oz/½ cup water
1½ tbsp Brewer's yeast

### 2nd dough

200g/7oz/1 cup plain white flour
50g/1¾oz/¼ cup malt flour
125ml/4fl oz/½ cup water
a pinch of salt
2 tbsp lard
6 tbsp extra virgin olive oil
½ tbsp Brewer's yeast
1 tsp malt

### And

2 tbsp extra virgin olive oil
plain white flour

**Preparation time:** 20 minutes
**Cooking time:** 15 minutes
**Difficulty:** easy

Prepare the first dough, putting flour, crumbled yeast and water into a food mixer; mix until you get a smooth lump. Place it in a bowl, cover with clingfilm and allow to rest for at least 90 minutes.

Pour both flours into a pile and place the leavened dough in the middle. Add lard, crumbled yeast, oil, salt, water and malt. Mix all the ingredients well and knead energically to get a soft and smooth dough. Roll out the dough slightly stretching it, fold it up and work with the palm of your hands to make a 5-6cm/2-2½ in thick roll. Brush with oil and allow to rest again for 1 hour. Heat the oven to 200°C/400°F/ Gas 6 and put a small saucepan containing water on the lower rack.

Place the roll on a semolina-floured surface and, using a spatula, cut it into small sticks (about 2cm/¾in thick). Lay them down on some semolina; take a piece at a time and slightly stretch it to get a pretty thick stick, about 18cm/7in long. Arrange the sticks on a baking tray, previously lined with greaseproof paper, and leave to rise for about 20 minutes. Bake for 15 minutes.

# Baguettes

## Ingredients
(1.5kg/3lb 5oz bread)

### 1st dough
800g/1lb 12oz/5¼ cups plain white flour
500ml/18fl oz/2¼ cups water
2 tbsp Brewer's yeast

### 2nd dough
300g/11oz/2 cups plain white flour
160ml/5½fl oz/¾ cup water
½ tbsp Brewer's yeast
1 tbsp salt

**Preparation time:** 50 minutes
**Cooking time:** 30 minutes
**Difficulty:** medium

Prepare the first dough, mixing the required ingredients (remember to use lukewarm water); leave to rise in a warm place for about 3 hours. At the end of the rising process, the dough volume should be tripled.

Once this dough is ready, add the flour, water, yeast and salt. Knead for 10-12 minutes, until smooth and elastic. Leave to rise for about 30 minutes, then shape it into small balls, about 35g/1¼oz/2 tbsp each.

Knead them for 20 minutes, then make the baguettes, rolling the balls from the middle to the outside in order to prevent air bubbles from appearing on the surface. Leave the baguettes to rise until they become well swollen but are still firm. Make 3 or 4 diagonal incisions on the top of each roll and bake at 200°C/400°F/Gas 6 for about 25-30 minutes.

**Note -** For a shinier baguette, brush the bread crust with water, before cooking.

# Wholemeal bread

## Ingredients
(700g/1lb 9oz bread)

### 1st dough
500g/1lb 2oz/3¼ cups plain white flour
225ml/8fl oz/1 cup water
1½ tbsp Brewer's yeast

### 2nd dough
50g/1¾ oz/¼ cup plain white flour
1 tbsp rye flour
1 tbsp spelt flour
1 tbsp corn meal
1 tbsp buckwheat flour
50g/1¾oz/¼ cup oats
135ml/4½fl oz/½ cup water
1 tsp Brewer's yeast

**Preparation time:** 45 minutes
**Cooking time:** 30 minutes
**Difficulty:** difficult

Prepare the first dough mixing flour, water and yeast, then leave to rise under a cloth for about 3 hours.

Sift the flours for the second dough and combine them with the first dough, the water and the yeast. Knead thoroughly to get an elastic and firm dough, then add the salt and the oats. Allow the dough to rest for about 40-50 minutes.

Cut into pieces, roll them (see photo 1) and after a few minutes shape them into loaves and place into small floured baskets (see photo 2). Leave to rise in a warm place for about 1 hour (until they double in volume and take the shape of the basket).

Place the loaves on baking trays and score their surfaces lengthwise. Bake at 220°C/425°F/Gas 7 until the bread turns brown.

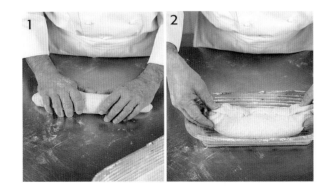

# Turinese breadsticks

## Ingredients
(40 breadsticks)

### *Breadsticks*
500g/1 lb 2 oz/3¼ cups plain white flour
250ml/9fl oz/1 cup water
1 tbsp butter
1 tsp Brewer's yeast
a pinch of salt
extra virgin olive oil

*Preparation time:* 30 minutes
*Cooking time:* 15 minutes
*Difficulty:* medium

Dissolve the yeast in lukewarm water and mix it with the flour; add melted, cool butter and salt. Work the dough to shape a ball; then make some rolls and leave them to rest on a floured surface for 15 minutes.

Slightly flatten them and brush with oil; cover with clingfilm and a cloth. When lightly puffed up, oil them again, gently press down and let rise again for 1 hour.

You'll get quite thick rolls (like a banana). Cut them into small pieces and stretch with your hands on a floured surface. Arrange them on a baking tray and leave to rise for 15 more minutes. Bake at 230°C/450°F/Gas 8 for 12-15 minutes.

*Tip -* These thin and crispy breadsticks are generally served as little snacks accompanied with finely sliced salami or creamy and velvet vegetable soups or again with raw vegetables, rich in liquids (such as lettuce, tomatoes, cucumbers…).

# Small rolls with peppers

## Ingredients
(500g/1lb 2oz bread)

### 1st dough
100g/3½oz/¾ cup plain white flour
50ml/2fl oz/¼ cup water
1 tsp Brewer's yeast

### 2nd dough
300g/11oz/2 cups plain white flour
240g/8½oz/1 cup red peppers, diced
160ml/5½fl oz/⅔ cup water
1 tbsp Brewer's yeast
a pinch of parsley
rye flour for dusting
a pinch of salt

**Preparation time:** 50 minutes
**Cooking time:** 20 minutes
**Difficulty:** medium

Prepare the first dough mixing flour, water and yeast. Leave to rise in a warm place under a cloth for about 3 hours.

Knead this dough with the remaining flour, water and yeast; halfway through the preparation add salt and parsley. When the dough is ready, add the peppers and knead briefly again. Allow to rest for about 1 hour.

Cut the dough into small pieces and roll them into balls. Arrange them on a baking tray and dust with rye flour. Bake at 230°C/450°F/Gas 8.

**Note -** Bread making is not as difficult as it may seem. You only have to know the right process and be able to choose the most suitable ingredients: first of all the yeast. The natural one (or sourdough) is usually used by bakers. Baking powder (or chemical yeast) is suitable for rolls that rise during baking. Brewer's yeast (in blocks or granular) is the most commonly used for home-made bread.

# Bread with pumpkin

## Ingredients
(700g/1lb 9oz bread)

### 1st dough
100g/3½ oz/¾ cup plain white flour
1 tsp Brewer's yeast

### 2nd dough
500g/1lb 2oz/3¼ cups plain white flour
280g/10oz/1¼ cups pumpkin, cleaned and baked
100ml/3½fl oz/½ cup water
50g/1¾oz/¼ cup sugar
½ tbsp butter
2 tbsp salt
2 tbsp Brewer's yeast

**Preparation time:** 50 minutes
**Cooking time:** 25 minutes
**Difficulty:** medium

Prepare the first dough mixing the required ingredients and enough water. Leave to rise at room temperature (about 26°C/79°F) for approximately 3 hours.

Knead the leavened dough with the remaining flour and the other ingredients. Bake and mash the pumpkin with a potato masher or a food mixer and add it to the dough. Allow it to rest for about 40 minutes.

Cut it into pieces, 250g/9oz each, and shape them as you like. Leave to rise at room temperature, sheltered from draughts, for 45-50 minutes. Bake at 220-230°C/425-450°F/Gas 7-8 for about 25 minutes.

# Bread with sunflower seeds

## Ingredients
(500g/1lb 2oz bread)

### 1st dough
100g/3½oz/¾ cup plain white flour
55ml/2fl oz/¼ cup water
1 tsp yeast

### 2nd dough
200g/7oz/1 cup plain white flour
100g/3½oz/¾ cup rye flour
150g/5½ oz/1 cup sunflower seeds
190ml/6½fl oz/¾ cup water
1 tbsp Brewer's yeast
rye flour for dusting
a pinch of salt

**Preparation time:** 45 minutes
**Cooking time:** 40 minutes
**Difficulty:** difficult

To prepare the first dough, mix flour, water and yeast and leave to rise under a cloth at room temperature for 3 hours.

Briefly toast the sunflower seeds, then knead all the ingredients required for the second dough, except for the salt and the sunflower seeds. When the dough is ready, add the sunflower seeds and knead it for some minutes more; leave to rise for 40-50 minutes.

Cut the dough into large and small pieces and roll into balls. After 10-15 minutes, gently make a cross in the larger balls (see photo 1) and arrange them on a baking tray.

Place the small balls of rolled dough in the centre of each cross (see photo 2). Lightly dust with rye flour and let rise under a cloth, sheltered from draughts, for 50-60 minutes. Bake at 220°C/425°F/Gas 7.

# The chef's utensils

1 **Extendable baking tray** - Made of non-stick material, it is the most innovative baking tray for pizza (but also for pies); if necessary, it stretches from 33cm/13in to 52cm/½in.

2 **Designer oil cruet** - When pizza is served warm and piping hot, a drizzle of oil at the last minute makes it even tastier. The stainless steel oil cruet looks nicer with a coloured handle and cap and it is the ideal vessel to keep chilli oil (which you can easily prepare by adding 4 or 5 red dried chillies to the oil and letting them settle in the oil cruet).

3 **Pizza turner** - The serrated cutting edge allows you to cut pizzas and flat breads as well as easily pick up the slices. It is also very handy to cut oven-baked pasta, lasagne or pies.

4 **Pizza cutting wheel** - The maxi wheel with the white handle is stylish and professional at the same time for slicing pizza without crumbling the crust, even when it's very crispy. It is a safe utensil thanks to its brass hand guard.

5 **Decorative pizza cutting wheel** - To make eating pizza a joyful time or to play a trick on your hungriest guests.

6 **Pizza plate** - If you want to recreate the characteristic atmosphere of a pizzeria at home, you must serve pizza on a large plate. This is undoubtedly the most suitable one.

7 **Salt grinder** - To get the most delicious focaccia, brush its holes with a fine extra virgin olive oil and dust it with some salt grains. Salt should be freshly ground with a plexiglas grinder, to prevent it from being too fine or too thick.

# Glossary

### "Aglio in camicia" (unpeeled garlic)
This definition refers to garlic cloves that are used without removing their peel in many recipes. Unpeeled garlic can be used both uncut or slightly crushed.

### Capocollo (Calabrese coppa)
This is a typical pork product of central-southern Italy made with the upper part of the neck and with part of the shoulder. It is similar to the Emilian coppa, however more delicate and more flavoured.

### Dicing
A slicing technique that requires in cutting vegetables into 5-7mm/¼ in cubes. If cubes are smaller, the right term is "brunoise"; if they are bigger the right expression is "to dice".

### Food processor or mixer
This is a domestic appliance used to mince, mix, pulverize and process different kinds of foods. A special three-bladed cutting attachment, driven by a powerful electric motor, turns at a thousand revolutions per minute.

### Fior di latte mozzarella
A kind of mozzarella cheese made from cow's milk; the low-fat version (with no more than 20% fat) and the light version (with between 20-35% fat) are both available.

### Hijiki algae
These algae are particularly suited to improve blood circulation. They are a very important source of calcium and the only ones containing vitamin B12. Before using, soak them in water for 15-30 minutes, so that they will increase to 4 or 5 times their size.

### Julienne
A slicing technique of cutting vegetables into very thin strips (2-3cm/¾-¼ in long and 1-2mm/¹/₁₂ in thick). This particular cut is usually hand-made with a knife; of course, you can also use a grater.

### Mandoline slicer (mandolina)
This is an utensil used to cut vegetables or fruits into a variety of different shapes (rings, julienne strips and so on). It is called mandoline because, using it, hands make a movement very similar to that of musicians playing the musical instrument.

## Marinade

Helps to both preserve and flavour foods. Marinades are very useful to eliminate the gamy flavour of meat and it is particularly suited for many fish dishes. Wine (both white and red), vegetables, spices and many other seasonings are usually used to prepare a marinade.

## Pasta maker

A manual utensil for domestic use that flattens pasta into different shapes and sizes. There's both an electric and a manual version (with a handle). Pasta can also be rolled with a rolling pin.

## Pastry board

A wooden board, smooth and perfectly flat, used to knead, stretch, roll and flatten pasta. As wood tends to warp with time, keep your pastry board in a dry place at an even temperature.

## Salt flakes

These flakes are sweeter than table salt and have the shape of small crystal flakes that easily break up in your hands. This type of salt is also known as Maldon salt.

## Stripping

Stripping means to remove the outer leaves (usually the most tattered) of vegetables or fruits, so as to use only the best inner ones.

## Tofu

A Chinese and Japanese speciality, produced from a milky liquid extracted from the soya (this is why it is also called soya cheese).

## "Trifolare"

"Trifolare" means slightly browning mushrooms in oil with parsley and garlic. This type of cooking is suited to almost every type of mushroom.

## Vaporizer

This is used to spray any liquid. Today it comes in a wide variety of types (gas or pump-action) and materials (plastic, aluminium, glass). It is also used to accurately and uniformly damp or grease the dough.

# Index